If I were to posture a guess, I'd guess that you have read in the Bible or heard from others that the most important command and instruction that God gave us was that we love Him with all of our heart, soul, mind, and strength. That God wants us to love Him with every single ounce of ourselves!

You are taking the time to read this book because you want to understand what that means, what it looks like, and how you can do it. I want you to know that God sees your desire, and He loves that you want to grow in this area. In the following chapters, we will dive into what kind of love this is, how you love someone not (no longer) physical, and what this looks like to live it out in all of its wonderful expressions.

Before we begin to dive into all of those wonderful questions, there is something so extremely vital and important that I need you to understand first. We can't begin to talk about any of those other questions and seek understanding until you understand this one thing... God already loves you and always has loved you with the greatest and most amazing love that this world has ever known!

We can't begin to properly love God back before realizing and recognizing this incredible truth. Since the very moment you were created, since the very moment He knit you in your mother's womb, God has loved you perfectly. Before you ever had a chance to do the right thing, to make the right choices, God loved you perfectly!

Before you ever made a mistake in your life, before you ever had a doubt about Him, before you ever ran away from Him, God loved you perfectly!

Before you ever intentionally did that thing, said that word, or thought that thought you knew was not right, God loved you perfectly!

Even after you have messed up and sinned in every conceivable way and you think there is no way that God could love you now, God still loves you perfectly EVEN THEN!

God has always loved you with an unconditional love that knows no bounds or limits. It's a greater love than any you have ever received from another person. There has never been a day where God has loved you any more or any less than He does right now. Not on your best day or worst day because God loves you not for what you do but for who you are.

You were created in His image, and you are so incredibly valued and worth so much to God. His love runs so deep for you that before you ever had a chance to know Him, God came to this earth in physical form to die on the cross for you. God the Father sent Jesus (God incarnate) to take our punishment for the sins we would commit. This one act of love, the greatest this world has ever seen, has opened up a way for you to spend eternity with Him.

This is God's heart and desire that you would have a perfect relationship restored with Him that would last forever. He wants you to be with Him in a perfect paradise lavished in His love. God wants His relationship with you closer and more intimate than it ever has been. This is His love that He freely shares with you!

So, let's take this time with a heart full of gratitude and appreciation and overflowing with His love for us and seek how we can love God back with all that we are!

Chapter 1

What kind of love is this?

There are a lot of things that we say we love.

We say we love our parents, our siblings, our children, and our spouse. We say we love our dog, our favorite food, our favorite restaurant, and our favorite place to vacation.

Obviously, what we mean when we say we love each of these things is different. The love is not the same kind of love nor is it to the same degree. The way we love our siblings is different from how we love our children. The way we love our spouse is certainly different from how we love our dog.

In the New Testament Greek there were a number of different words that we translate to the English word "love." You could tell if it was a friendship kind of love, an erotic love, a deep profound love, or a love for a family member just by looking at which of the words was used.

So how, then, are we to love God? What kind of love is this? What should our relationship with Him look like?

The answer, although not as simple as you might be hoping for, is even better than we first imagined. You see, we serve a triune God. That means that God is both three and one. He is the Father, Son, and Holy Spirit.

How we relate to the one true God is, therefore, triune as well. We are to love God with all of our heart, soul, mind, and strength but the kind of love and relationship we have with God the Father, God the Son, and God the Holy Spirit may all be a little different. As you will see and experience, this is an incredible blessing for us. Let's dive a little deeper!

For many, thinking of, interacting with, and talking to God the Father in prayer is a real, genuine fatherly relationship. There is a recognition of the care and provision provided by God. There is reverent respect and love, knowing that God is looking out for us, protecting us, and desiring to guide us in our lives. We understand that, when necessary, God will discipline/correct us because, out of His love for us, He wants to redirect us away from trouble.

If you had a great earthly father, this connection and love for God the Father will flow effortlessly. It is everything you have come to know and love in your earthly father only perfected.

If you have learned more from your earthly father's example of how not to be a good parent or if you did not have a father figure growing up, this relationship with God may take a little longer to grow. God is patient and understanding as you work through this learning curve with Him. Do not worry or fret. Trust God and lean into this relationship earnestly and it will grow deeper day by day.

Your relationship with Jesus, God the Son, may have a different flavor to it. Your relationship may be less father figure and more best friend. Throughout the Gospels, Jesus showed Himself to be a friend of sinners and one who would walk the journey with those who were seeking to be with Him and learn from Him. He is our best friend in times of trouble, loneliness, and despair. He is there to lean on, converse with, and live life with.

The Bible says that no temptation experienced by man is foreign to Jesus. He lived and walked on this broken earth just as we do, so now we have a High Priest (and best friend) who truly understands what we are going through. This is not to think less of the perfect holiness, power, and authority that Jesus possesses but to think of Him in humility and awe that He would come to live with us, suffer with and for us, and die for us. Jesus is our friend who is willing and did lay down His life for ours.

The third part of the Godhead is the Holy Spirit. Our relationship with Him may take the form and flavor of Him as our counselor and guide. It is He who came when Jesus ascended back up into Heaven to sit at the right hand of God the Father, and it is He who dwells within us when we come to saving faith in Christ.

The Holy Spirit convicts us when we start to wander off the path that God is calling us to follow. He lays it upon our hearts when we need to change course and encourages us when we are headed the right way. We can turn to Him in prayer, knowing that He has been with us through it all. He is our intercessor with the Father, and it is through Him that we are able to have the strength and courage to keep moving in what the Father has called us to.

All of these relationships will grow over time and subtly change as we come to know God better. We will understand the richness and blessing of the Trinity as we fall deeper in love with Him, and our appreciation will only continue to grow.

Trying to understand the Trinity and wrap your mind around this all can be very difficult, especially when you are just starting out on your journey of faith. I want to encourage you to have conversations and ask questions with those who are mature Christians in your life and to find a mentor to walk this journey with you.

I know that as you continue this walk, God will continue to reveal Himself to you more and more. There may not be a point where you can explain exactly how all of it works, but I am 100% confident you will someday reach a point where you can say that you have personally experienced God the Father, God the Son, and God the Holy Spirit in your life and you know Him to be true beyond a doubt.

Reflect on some questions that can help us grow in our understanding and application of God's love:

1. How do you personally experience God's love in your life? How does it make you feel and act?

2. How do you express your love for God in your daily life? What are some ways that you show Him your gratitude, devotion, and obedience?

3. How do you share God's love with others? How do you demonstrate His love to your family, friends, neighbors, and strangers?

4. How do you overcome the challenges and obstacles that may hinder your love for God? How do you deal with doubts, fears, temptations, and sins that may affect your relationship with Him?

5. How do you grow in your knowledge and intimacy with God? What are some practices or habits that help you deepen your connection and communication with Him?

Chapter 2

How do I love someone not (no longer) physical?

You know God loves you and desires for you to love Him with all of your heart. You are beginning to wrap your mind around what kind of love this is as you interact with God the Father, Jesus, and the Holy Spirit. Now, the question is: How do I actually show this love to God?

We are used to showing our love to those who are physically with us. This is our default situation and what most of us have known all of our lives. We know how to give great big bear hugs, say a kind word when we see the signs that our loved one is hurting, and express our love through an act of service that touches their heart, like making them dinner or doing their least favorite chore for them.

Now, of course, we don't only love the people who are physically in the same room as us. Our love doesn't cease merely because physical distance has occurred.

You might be thinking right now about the loved ones in your life who have passed away. Surely you still love them even though they are no longer physically here. Yet this situation is not quite the same. You might be thinking of the long-distance relationship you once had (or are currently in) or the family member living in another state you cherish seeing at the holidays. You love that person deeply even though you may be across the country or across the world from them, and yet that situation doesn't seem quite the same either.

What makes your relationship with God different from any of those relationships is that God is alive and with you at all times through His Holy Spirit. This can boggle our minds at first because we really don't have a category like that with anyone else. We are used to people needing to be with us physically to spend all day with them, let alone all week, all month, or all of our lives.

You see, there is no being lonely like there is with loving someone who has passed. Jesus is with you, and He has promised He will NEVER leave you nor forsake you. He isn't going anywhere! On top of that, God's never going to stop speaking to you, and He desires for you to talk with Him daily as your relationship grows stronger and closer.

It's different from your long-distance relationship because you get to share every single bland, exciting, and intimate moment of your life with God and not just the moments on the phone or video chat. It's not just Thanksgiving and birthday celebrations that are spent together. Twenty-four hours a day, seven days a week, God is there with you. He may not be able to be physically seen, but He is no less there with you because of it.

So, what does it look like to love the God who is always present in spirit? What are some of the different ways that we can express our love for our great and amazing God?

What we are about to see is that when we love someone, we talk to them and about them. We want to get to know everything about them and spend time together. We share meals and life together. We show love and respect to the people they love and care about and want to get to know them as well. When we really truly love someone, we will do anything for them.

These ring true in your existing relationships and shine brightly in how the Bible calls us to love God! Let's take each aspect and dive in a little deeper!

Reflect on this chapter using the following questions:

1. What makes your relationship with God different from any of those relationships?

2. What are some of the challenges or benefits of loving a God who is not physical?

Chapter 3

PRAYER

When we love someone, we talk to them.

When the word 'prayer' gets mentioned, it probably conjures up an image of something in your mind. Maybe it's the formal prayers that you have heard word for word spoken by many different people over your lifetime. Maybe it's the image of those "really holy" people you know knelt down on their knees with their hands clasped together who speak so intensely. For some, what comes to mind might be the people in their lives who just seem to pray so effortlessly these beautiful prayers that always seem to touch our hearts in the way we need in that moment. There are many different types and ways to pray, and that can become really overwhelming.

Let's take all of those past experiences and things we think we know about prayer and just put them aside for the time being, though, and drill down to what the heart of prayer really is. Prayer is simply an ongoing conversation that you have with God!

One of the great joys of parenthood is when your child snuggles up close to you on the couch, and you get to put your arm around them, hold them, and just talk with them. You enjoy their company and get to talk with them about how their day or week is going while trying to guide them through the difficult situations that have come their way.

God looks at us, His children and says, "Draw closer to me and share with me everything that is on your heart. Tell me about all of the big and little things that have brought you joy and have made you worry. Find comfort in me and trust that I am always with you."

God wants us to come to Him with every piece of our day, whether we think it is trivial or life-changing (sometimes we don't know which events are which until long after the fact anyway). He wants us to share our joys with Him, our sorrows, worries, and concerns as well. He wants to hear about our desires and the people we care about.

There isn't a special way that we need to do this. There is nothing we need to memorize or anything that we need to say at specific times of the day. What God cares about is that you are speaking from the heart to Him because you love and cherish the time you share in conversation!

I love spending time with God and talking with Him all throughout the day. Sometimes it is a dedicated time of prayer where I find a nice quiet spot to be alone with God, but often it is in the car while driving, while taking the dog for a walk, or working on something in the house. Sometimes, the time spent is 30-45 minutes, but most of my prayers are just two or three sentences. I like to check in with Him and share little things with Him throughout the day, and I have learned over the years to stop and ask God as many questions as possible. Why should I try to figure things out on my own when I can trust and rely on the One who knows all things?!

Conversation/prayer with God is not a monologue, though. How infuriating would it be if you had a friend who always called you, said everything they wanted to say, and then said "bye" and hung up before you could get a word in? When we speak to God and finish by saying "amen" and immediately getting back to what we were doing before, this is what we are doing to Him. Don't do that! You are missing out on so many blessings that come through hearing what our Heavenly Father is trying to teach us.

As any loving father or parent would do, God is always speaking into our lives to try to guard us away from harm and to set us on the best path for our lives. He does this through the written Word He has preserved for us and He does that through times of prayer when we sit still and listen for Him.

God's not a shouter, though. He is tender, gentle, and patient, seeking to speak in a whisper that we must lean in to hear. He could speak with a loud booming voice that all the world could hear at once, but instead, He chooses the tone that makes us lean in and draw close to hear and understand.

Why does God choose to speak to His children in this way? Because He loves us and wants to have a close, intimate relationship with us! What kind of relationship would it be if both parties only ever shouted over long distances to each other? It's difficult to imagine being close or special in any way.

Make room in your life and in your times conversing with God to speak and to listen, to share and to hear. There are times that I set aside to come to God in prayer where I don't say much, if anything, at all. Just sitting down to spend time thinking about God and His goodness and love is one of the most calming and peaceful things we can do during our day. We don't need an agenda before we spend time talking with a friend. We just know we love to spend time with them and every conversation is a blessing. It is the same way with God.

One of the best ways we can love someone is by taking the time and making it a priority to talk with them and actively listen when they speak. Pause your reading for a little and just talk with God right now like you would talk to your parent or best friend. Pour out everything that is on your heart and rest in His presence as He replies back to you, the son or daughter He so dearly loves!

If, in doing so, you have experienced the blessing that prayer is and have been moved to renew your focus on it, please use the simple tool included in the back of this book to help you increase your dialog with God. Just as we can easily get caught up in the busyness of life and drift apart from friends, this can happen with God as well. Be intentional in making a plan to spend more time with Him, and you will be so glad that you did!

Reflect on this chapter using the following questions:

1. How do you feel about prayer?

2. What is one thing that you learned or want to apply from this lesson?

3. What is one thing that you want to learn more or improve about prayer?

4. How can you help or encourage someone else to pray?

Chapter 4

Evangelism

When you love someone, you talk about them.

Ever talked to someone who is in a brand-new relationship or just got engaged or married? Of course, you have! What did that person talk about? There is almost a one hundred percent chance that they talked about their significant other at some point. When we really love someone, we simply can't help but to talk about them!

Whether it's our girlfriends/boyfriends, fiancés, spouses, kids, or pets, we love to share with others how awesome the people are who we love the most. Scan down through your Facebook feed or other social media platform of choice, and you will find post after post of people sharing their love for the important people in their lives. When we love God with all of our heart, soul, mind, and strength, we can't help but talk about Him as well!

In church, we like to use big, fancy words for things. Sometimes, it helps to bring clarity to have really specific words but oftentimes it just causes confusion. I prefer to keep things as simple as possible. Evangelism is just a fancy way of saying, "talking to people about how awesome God is and how much we love Him."

When we come to know Jesus as the Lord and Savior of our lives, we learn something amazing about this God we serve. We learn that He wants to have a close, personal relationship with us. We learn that He is loving, patient, merciful, compassionate, forgiving, kind, gentle, trustworthy, strong, just, and faithful. We learn that His love is perfect and never waivers and that He proved that to us on the cross. God loves us so much that He would willingly die an excruciating death on the cross so that He could overcome and defeat death to pave the way for us to be with Him for all of eternity. We learn that through faith in Christ, this opportunity is made available to all of us regardless of any mistakes or failures we have made in our lives!

When we learn all of that and believe it in our hearts, how could we possibly keep that in?!

What better, more exciting news could we ever share with someone? Don't hold it in; let it out!

Tell your friends, family members, co-workers, and neighbors about how awesome God is. Tell them about the special time you got to spend with Him over the weekend and the amazing conversation you had with Him when you finished reading the previous chapter. Share with them about how special it is to be fully known and yet still fully loved by God and how comforting it is to be able to be honest and real with no walls up as you open up to God.

At the heart of all of this Good News that we have with God in this new relationship with Him is that this relationship can be had by others as well! No one can have the same relationship I have with my spouse, my kids, or even my dog, but you can have the relationship I have with Jesus. In fact, I WANT you to have that same relationship, and we can all be friends together, making it even more awesome!

So, how is talking about God one of the ways that we love God? Have you ever seen the face of your spouse, kids, or friends when you brag about how awesome they are and how much you love them to others? Do you remember how you felt the last time that you were on the receiving end of someone you care about talking glowingly of you?

When somebody does this, it means the world to us. It puts us in a great mood for the rest of the day, and few things make us feel more loved than when someone goes out of their way to verbalize to others how much we are loved and appreciated.

When we talk to others about God, it glorifies and honors Him. It brings joy to Him to hear our love for Him expressed, and He uses that to draw His other children closer to Him. When we really love someone, we can't help but talk about them, so pause before going on to the next chapter and let someone know about how awesome God is!

Stir up yourself to commit to sharing more with others. Tell them what God can do for them and what He has done in your life. Use the "My Life Recorder" tool in the back of the book to help you track your progress on your commitment.

Reflect on this chapter using the following questions:

1. How do you feel about talking about God?

2. What is one thing that you learned or want to apply from this lesson?

3. What is one thing that you want to learn more or improve about talking about God?

4. How can you help or encourage someone else to talk about God?

26

Chapter 5

Discipleship

When we love someone, we want to learn everything about them.

Favorite food? ONE, TWO, THREE, GO!

Did you shout it out? How many times have we had these fun back and forth conversations with others as we are getting to know them? It starts off in the beginning with really fun, silly questions, and over time, the questions dive deeper and deeper.

Getting to know someone is one of the ways we show that we care about and love them. In fact, the more effort and time we spend getting to know someone is one of the best ways to gauge how much we actually care. How much time have you spent getting to know your spouse compared to your barber? How about your best friend compared to those awesome men and women who come pick up your trash each week when you set it at the curb? If you have a dog, right now you could most likely even tell me all of the things they like to eat or don't like, all of their favorite toys, the things that scare them, and their favorite places and times to take a nap. For those whom we love, we will spend as much time as it takes to know them as well as possible, and we will enjoy every second of it!

In our relationship with God, our getting to know each other is a little different because it is one-sided. God already knows us completely, better than we even know ourselves. Mark this page and read Psalm 139 before continuing to see for yourself!

We still have the blessing of learning about God, though, and He was kind enough to reveal Himself to us in a book (the Bible) that we can take with us and read wherever we are. These words are not static reminders of a past God, though, but are the words that the living God speaks into your life and the circumstances you are walking through today.

God reveals Himself through the interactions with His people throughout the Old and New Testaments. God shows who He is as He relates to the Israelites through all of their ups and downs. We learn what brings joy, anger, and jealousy to Him through the Law. In the New

Testament, we are blessed to learn from Jesus in bodily form as to what it looks like to live perfectly in obedience to the will of God. God came down to earth, and He demonstrated this for us so we could learn even more about Him. But He also did this so we could learn what we are called to be and do as well.

Jesus calls us to follow Him and be His disciples. That means we not only learn about Him, but we also learn to walk in His footsteps as His apprentices. He is both the subject of our learning and the teacher as well. To get to know Jesus is to get to know who we will be as we are formed into His likeness as we grow deeper in our faith and journey with Him.

What pleases God and reveals our hearts is how serious we take getting to know Him and how intentional we are in doing so. We can study the Word He has given us to the deepest possible depths and never stop learning. There are a lot of great Bible dictionaries, commentaries, and books that dedicated Christians have written and compiled to help us understand what God is revealing of Himself. Use these great tools and invite others to study God's Word with you.

One of the best things we can do to learn about God through His Word is to take time after reading it to spend with Him in prayer and to seek to hear His voice. We can ask Jesus to speak loud and clear and answer our prayers to know what it is that He wants us to learn and how we can apply it to our lives.

Jesus said to be disciples and make disciples, disciplined followers, of everyone. Did you know we are always making disciples? When we teach our children about life, we are making disciples. When we teach our children about life with Jesus, we are making them disciples of Christ.

People learn from each other all the time; we always impact those around us. How we live our lives, walk with God, love Him, and rely on Him sets an example for others. We ought to be intentional about this. Intentionally living for and with God is being a disciple. Intentionally helping others to live for and with God is making disciples of Jesus.

Close this book and take some time right now to think through how you can be a more disciplined follower of Jesus. Think about how you can help others to be disciplined followers of Christ. Let's be intentional! What is one thing you could begin doing this week to take the next step on that journey? Be as specific as possible as to what it is and when you will do it, and begin tracking your success in the "My Life Recorder" tool at the end of this book. Allow it to become a part of the daily rhythm of your life!

Reflect on this chapter using the following questions:

1. How do you intend to be a disciplined follower of God?

2. How do you study the Bible and what tools or methods do you use?

3. Who are you influencing to walk with God?

4. Who would you like to influence? How do you share God's love and truth with them?

5. How do you track your progress and goals in this learning journey? Have you used "My Life Recorder"? How did it help you or why not?

Chapter 6

Breaking of Bread

When we love someone, we share meals and life together.

Eating together is a vital part of connecting to others. As I was growing up, my family had a lot of traditions that were based around the food we had at family gatherings. We had the normal meals around Easter, Thanksgiving, Christmas, and New Year's Day but birthdays also had a special dietary ritual.

For everyone's birthdays, the whole family would gather together, and the food was always the same: sloppy joes (barbeque sandwiches) and potato chips. Every year for every age for every person. Now, there is nothing special about sloppy joes and chips if you are unfamiliar with them. They are a very common food eaten all the time by both children and adults where I'm from, yet every time I eat that meal, I can't help but feel like it must be someone's birthday and think back to fond memories. The food transcends the nutritional value it holds and transports me mentally and emotionally to a different place and time. That silly common meal holds a very special place in my heart because of those who have shared the table with me eating it and because of the love that went into preparing it each time.

Jewish people observe Shabbat, often setting aside Friday night to gather for a God-centered meal. More and more followers of Jesus are experiencing the benefit of sharing meals with others, intentionally including God as part of the meal. Jesus said, where 2 or 3 are gathered in His name, there He is in the midst. Let's do it! Let's take the opportunity to share meals with other believers instead of focusing on politics, work or just fun. Let's intentionally focus on a God-honoring time together.

God gave the Israelites a very special meal to observe when He rescued them out of slavery in Egypt. As part of the Old Covenant, they were to keep the Passover meal every year as a remembrance of what God had done and what He promised He would do. The meal was a family meal shared with loved ones and the God they so dearly loved.

On the night in which Jesus was betrayed, Jesus gathered together His disciples for a very special Passover observance that Christians call the Last Supper. All of the normal traditions of that meal were observed but Jesus graciously gave us a way in the New Covenant to commune with Him until He comes again.

Jesus broke bread and told the disciples that this bread was His body that was to be sacrificed for them, and the cup He held up was the new covenant in His blood. In doing so, the common elements of bread and wine/juice were elevated to new meaning and significance in the lives of all who would be followers of Jesus from that time on.

For us today, the breaking of bread and the drinking of the cup as part of the act of holy communion is something sacred and preciously held. It's a family meal we share with brothers and sisters in Christ around the table. Perhaps it's part of a service or part of a meal that is shared with the intention to honor God. It's a transporting of us back to that table of the last supper as we join in with Jesus and His disciples. It's a joining with one another and also fellow Christians around the world and back through the generations as we all share in communion with Christ.

Some people offer communion as part of holiday and family gatherings. After all, the Lord's Supper is a proclamation of His death until He comes again. Some people share at their gatherings the Good News of Jesus' sacrifice and invite those to partake of the Lord's Supper who recognize Jesus as Lord and Savior.

There is a nourishment to our souls that far exceeds the caloric intake of bread and fruit of the vine. We are sustained for life through our communion with Christ. There is so much richness to the blessing of communion that Jesus gave to us that we tend to grow to understand it and appreciate it more as the years of our lives pass by.

There is nothing in this life that quite compares to the breaking of bread around the table with fellow believers as we commune together with Christ. It is as if He is sitting at the table with us in those moments, and we share a meal and our lives with our Lord and each other.

At some point this week, share this sacred meal with Jesus and fellow believers. Share it often as the joy of being close to the Lord will only grow as your relationship with Him deepens. Show your love to God as you live your life together with Him and others in community and common unity, gathering together for the breaking of bread.

Is this an area to commit to or renew your commitment? Track your progress with the tool in the back, "My Life Recorder".

Reflect on this chapter using the following questions:

1. What is a memorable meal that you have shared with someone? How did it affect your relationship?

2. How can you more regularly eat with fellow believers? What are the similarities and differences between the Passover and the Lord's Supper?

3. What do they teach us about God and HIs salvation? How can you pray, talk, and share the Lord's Supper this week at home or with other believers?

4. How can you invite someone who does not know Jesus to share a meal with you? How can you show them God's love and truth? How can you explain the Lord's Supper to them?

Chapter 7

Love Others As Yourself

When we love someone, we show love and respect to the people they love and care about.

Next time you are having a conversation with a single parent, ask them what criteria they are looking for in someone before they begin to date them. Take notice of how quickly they mention how any prospective partner must love and care about their children. It's non-negotiable for almost every single parent. Why? You can't love someone without loving and caring about the people that they love with all their heart!

As we seek to love God, we have to understand who the people are whom God loves with all of His heart. The Bible tells us that God formed each one of us uniquely in His image, and each and every one of us holds a special place in His heart. Regardless of how much we have sinned and how long we may have rebelled against Him, God still loves each one of us so greatly that He gave His life for us. Every single person you have ever met or will ever meet is a person that God loves with all of His heart. Every single person has immense worth and value in God's eyes because they are His.

If we are going to have a sincere personal relationship with God, we must love **ALL** of those that He loves!

What does doing this look like during our daily walk? It looks like love being poured out on others continuously. Every time we interact with someone, we are called to treat them the way that we would want to be treated. Not just what we would consider okay or satisfactory for the situation, but that we would go above and beyond whenever we see the opportunity.

Loving others looks like slowing down and taking the time to really listen to someone as they talk about their day or what they are going through in that season of life. Loving others looks like stopping what you are doing to give someone else a hand. It's knowing you have no obligation to help but doing so anyways because you want to brighten that person's day. It's saying you are so valuable and of such worth in God's eyes that I will show you great honor and respect with my time.

Loving others looks like our hearts rejoicing when others are filled with joy and our hearts breaking when others are broken. Loving others is celebrating their achievements just as much as you'd celebrate your own. It's sitting beside someone and holding them or crying with them when a loved one passes away. When we love others, we enter into their lives and are present with them through the ups and downs.

Loving others looks like radical generosity. It's seeing everything we have (time, talent, and treasure) as a resource given to us by God for us to hold on to as loosely as possible until God shows us an opportunity to use it. It is seeing every resource as a potential blessing to someone else. It is the giving and pouring out of ourselves beyond societal norms to show that the other person means more to you than they realize.

Jesus said that the command to love others was second only to the command for complete love and devotion to God. It is that important to God that you love those whom He loves!

Be intentional in looking for opportunities each day to show others your love for them through your use of the time, talent, and treasure that God have given to you to manage. Take some time in prayer with God right now to recognize specific opportunities you have coming up this week to be more loving to others. Is there a certain person or group of people that you would like to focus on this week? It will take time for us to grow more loving, but we can begin to take the steps today!

Track your progress with the "My Life Recorder" at the end of the book.

Reflect on this chapter using the following questions:

1. Who has shown you love and kindness in a meaningful way? How did they make you feel and reflect God's love?

2. What are the characteristics of love and the fruit of the Spirit in 1 Corinthians 13:4-7 and Galatians 5:22-23? Which ones do you need to grow in?

3. Who are some people that you want to show more love to? How can you show them love this week?

4. How can you use your time, talent, or treasure to love others as yourself? Who and how can you bless with your resources?

5. How do you track your progress in loving others as yourself? Have you used the "My Life Recorder" tool? How did it help you or why not?

Chapter 8

Fellowship

When we love someone, we want to really get to know the people that are a part of their life.

As dating turns to engagement, wedding plans are made, and preparations begin for the big day. Many conversations occur to discuss colors, flowers, songs, and all of the other details of the beautiful wedding. The happy couple talks about dreams of a life together and what the future may hold for them.

Imagine in the course of those conversations that one partner turns to the other and says, "I will always go out of my way to not only love you with all my heart, but I will also love your family and friends as well anytime we happen to be in the same place or the same room, BUT I'm never going to make any effort to really get to know them well."

What do you think the odds are that the person hearing that statement will feel loved and treasured by their future spouse? Imagine being in that position and having someone who claims they love you tell you that it is not important to them to get to know the people who are the closest to you in your life and mean so much to you! I don't know about you, but if it's me in that position, I'd be really questioning how real that person's love is for me. When we truly love someone, we want to really get to know the people that are a part of their life.

If we say we love God, we should want to get to know others well to live in community with them, committing to love each other and to, together, serve others.

Being a follower of God and loving God was never meant to be a solo sport. In the beginning, God created Adam but saw that it was good that he should not be alone. We were meant to live in community with God and within a community of people whom He loves, who know each other to their core and are intentional in walking out life and ministry together.

Fellowship isn't just a meal together or a fun church outing to a baseball game or miniature golf (even if they are a lot of fun). Real, genuine fellowship is so much more than that.   It is common unity. It takes time and effort over time to learn to love and serve God. It's knowing those whom God put around you in your life in the deepest ways possible.

Because we love God, we take the time to know whom He loves at a level far beneath the surface. More than just learning their likes and dislikes, we become intentional to get to know their deepest fears and most cherished dreams. We come to know their struggles in each season, and we recognize when they need encouragement and prayer just by the look on their face. We learn what is on their hearts and the things they are praying the hardest for in their lives and we pray those prayers with them. We celebrate the victories of the day and their growth in Christ through the seasons. When we love God, we tell Him (and back it up with action) that since these are people whom You love, we will do everything within our power and ability to go out of our way to be present in their lives with compassion, care, and concern at every turn.

We commit to nurturing the relationship. And we learn how to serve the Lord together, learning how to fit together as we serve God.

Texts and emails are great ways to check in with someone, but take some time today to be intentional in reaching out verbally to someone. Have a conversation in person over a cup of coffee or slice of pizza, or give someone a call and take the lead by really opening up about yourself. Be vulnerable in your openness and create a safe space where they may follow suit.

Start today! Extend your circle, deepen your commitment to others, and reach out to someone! Pray for wisdom and guidance for the next step God is calling you to, and then track your progress with the "My Life Recorder" tool in the back of the book.

Reflect on this chapter using the following questions:

1. Who is close to God and close to you? How do they show their love for God and for you? How do they inspire you to love God and others more?

2. What do Hebrews 10:24-25 and Acts 2:42-47 teach us about the importance and benefits of

fellowship? How can we apply these verses to our lives today?

3. Who are some people that you want to get to know better? How can you reach out and connect with them this week?

4. How can you use your time, talent, or treasure to love others and serve God? Who and how can you bless with your resources?

5. How do you track your progress in loving God and others, and getting to know them well? Have you used the "My Life Recorder" tool? How did it help you or why not?

Chapter 9

Mission/Calling

When we love someone, we are honored to be a part of their story.

I know a guy named Rauly Jimenez who has an awesome heart for God (he actually volunteered to design this book cover for me!). He is growing in his faith, pushing himself out of his comfort zone, and sharing the Gospel with people in-person and online.

As I walked with him through my first book, "Becoming Jesus' Apprentice", it became really obvious that Rauly had a unique mission and calling in his walk with God. God was calling him to make video games that would plant seeds and lead people to Christ! He has a God-given dream that one day, the work that the Holy Spirit produces through him in the form of a video game would touch the hearts of people who may have never stepped inside of a church or never have been open to hearing the Gospel. How cool is that?!

Seeing Rauly's heart, passion, and vision continually inspires me. I see how God is working through him and the potential of what could be, and all I want to do is help make it a reality! Now, unfortunately for Rauly, I'm about as technologically advanced as a 5th grader, but that doesn't stop me from wanting to do anything I can, however small it may be, to help. This is Rauly's story, and I am just honored to play the smallest of parts in it.

God's story is the story of redemption. God has set out to redeem His creation from their sins through their faith and trust in Jesus as Lord and Savior, and this story will end just as Revelation says, with God's people once again living in perfect paradise with him.

You and I, we get to be small characters in that story. We are not the main character, but we are also by no means just extras in God's eyes. We are special to Him, created uniquely in His image, and because of that, each of us has a unique calling and part to play in the story of God's redemption of humanity.

All of your talents, skills, and abilities were given to you for a special purpose. All of the interests and passions you have were planted there by God. All of the experiences you have gone through in your life have shaped and molded you to prepare you for the thing that only you are uniquely called to do in this time and place. As we discussed earlier, we all have a general calling to make disciples, but you have a special, unique calling as well!

What does that look like? For Rauly, it meant using his passion for playing video games and his skills as a developer to dedicate himself to creating a Christian video game. For my buddy "GOOGGZ," it means taking his love and skill in producing music and years in the music industry and beginning to produce music meant to turn the hearts of people towards God. For my friend Dan, it meant taking the skills he learned growing up playing the organ and piano and using that for a lifetime of leading others into close, personal worship of God. For Ralph, it meant coming alongside a crazy pastor (me!) to start an online church and discipling network. For Brendan, it meant taking the lessons he learned as a father and starting "Slingshot eSports" to create an environment through video game outreaches to connect parents to their children and children to God. For John, it meant using his love of God and

70+ years of life experiences and learning to start a microchurch, leading people to Christ through his door-to-door invitations. For Lizzy, it means a calling to take her love of plants and transform that into a community garden producing free food for anyone who needs it.

So, what is your calling? How does someone know? These examples I listed may all sound completely different, but they all hold one thing in common: listening to the promptings of the Holy Spirit. God is already speaking it into your life and onto your heart. He wants you to be a part of His story. Do you want to be a part of His?

Take time today to pray with God. As you sit in His presence, bring to God those things that make your heart leap for joy when you do them, as well as the things that break your heart when you witness them. Our unique calling is often tied to one of these two things, as God created our hearts to respond so strongly in these areas.

It's time to do a new thing and serve God in a new way because when we recognize who He is and what He has done/is doing, how can we desire anything else other than to be a part of it?

When we love someone, we are honored to be a part of their story.

What is your unique ministry? If you are not sure, make it a focus of prayer and discovery to find out.

Write down the steps you need to take to fulfill your ministry. Then, every day, try to take a Ministry Step. Note your progress in the "My Life Recorder" tool.

Reflect on this chapter using the following questions:

1. What makes your heart leap for joy when you do it or think about it?

2. What breaks your heart to see or think about?

3. What gifts, talents, and abilities do you possess?

4. Have you felt the Holy Spirit already calling you to serve God in a unique way?

Chapter 10

How To Make Disciples

Do you know anyone who is a hoarder? Hoarders collect more and more things, creating huge stockpiles of objects, but hardly ever use them or share them with others. Don't hoard the knowledge you have learned throughout this book! Put it into practice and lead others to understand and practice these things with you. In doing so, you are helping to make that person a disciple of Christ as well!

When Jesus was about to depart this world and ascend back up into Heaven, He left a simple instruction (the Great Commission) to His disciples and everyone who was a follower of His. Instructions so simple that every follower of His could do it regardless of who they were, how long they had been following Him, or how much formal education that they had received. Jesus told them to just go and makes disciples, baptize them, and teach them what they had already learned.

Now, I know that can sound confusing and overwhelming but it shouldn't! What you have learned in the preceding chapters is the essence of making disciples. It is not complicated and an excellent foundation to start your journey with God and an excellent foundation for others to begin their journey as well. Pray about who God is leading you to share your life with. Think about all the different groups of people you are connected to. God is calling you to be a messenger of Good News to some of them! Invite someone from each group to read the book with you or through informal conversations, invite them to do what you have learned, one chapter at a time. Invite others to participate with you in living out chapters three through nine. And, don't forget to encourage each other to find the special areas of service God has for you. He has special things for all of us! As you do these things, you are being obedient to what Jesus called all of His followers to do! You will be making disciples. You got this!

Reflect on this chapter using the following questions:

1. Who is God laying on your heart that you need to share this with next?

2. What groups of people are you regularly in contact with? Family? Friends? Coworkers? Neighbors? Clubs/Hobby groups?

3. Read Matthew 28:18-20. How can you start each day with this being your mission? What can you do to not lose focus of it throughout the day?

My Life Recorder

Without a step-by-step plan, our best-laid intentions become New Year's resolutions that get renewed on an ongoing basis but never accomplished. Small, specific, measurable goals are the key to sustained progress in anything. Learning what it means to love God and grow in that daily is certainly worth every ounce of effort that we can pour into it.

On the following pages are copies of a daily tool called the "My Life Recorder" developed by Kingdom Inc. It is an awesome tool to help us take our goals and turn them into actionable plans so that we can see our progress as we grow in our walk and are obedient to what God is calling us to.

The recorder takes the seven days of the week and gives space for four foundational categories to be tracked each day. Those categories are "spent time with God. "light to someone in darkness", "time with others growing in God", and "helped/ministered to someone and/or took a ministry step".

At the end of each day, go through each of the categories and circle the level in which you feel that you accomplished. At the end of the week, total up the results to keep track of your weekly progress. An example is included to help you get started.

On the opposite page from the recorder is space for you to write specific goals you would like to do in order to grow in each of the four categories.

Maybe it's to spend more time with God or talk to Him more. Maybe it is showing love to God by loving those whom He loves and getting to know them on their deepest levels. Whatever area you feel you're called to work on next, make sure to make your goal as specific as possible. "Taking ten minutes to pray after breakfast" is much more helpful than "pray more" as a goal. "Start a conversation about faith with a coworker" is much better than just "share the Gospel." It's even better if you can list the specific coworker you have in mind. Make it small, specific, and measurable, and then celebrate with God every time you are obedient to what He has called you to grow in!

In chapters three through nine of this book, we covered seven different things that we do when we love someone and what that means in our love of God. Pray about these, and let them be an inspiration as you set goals and seek to grow in your faith.

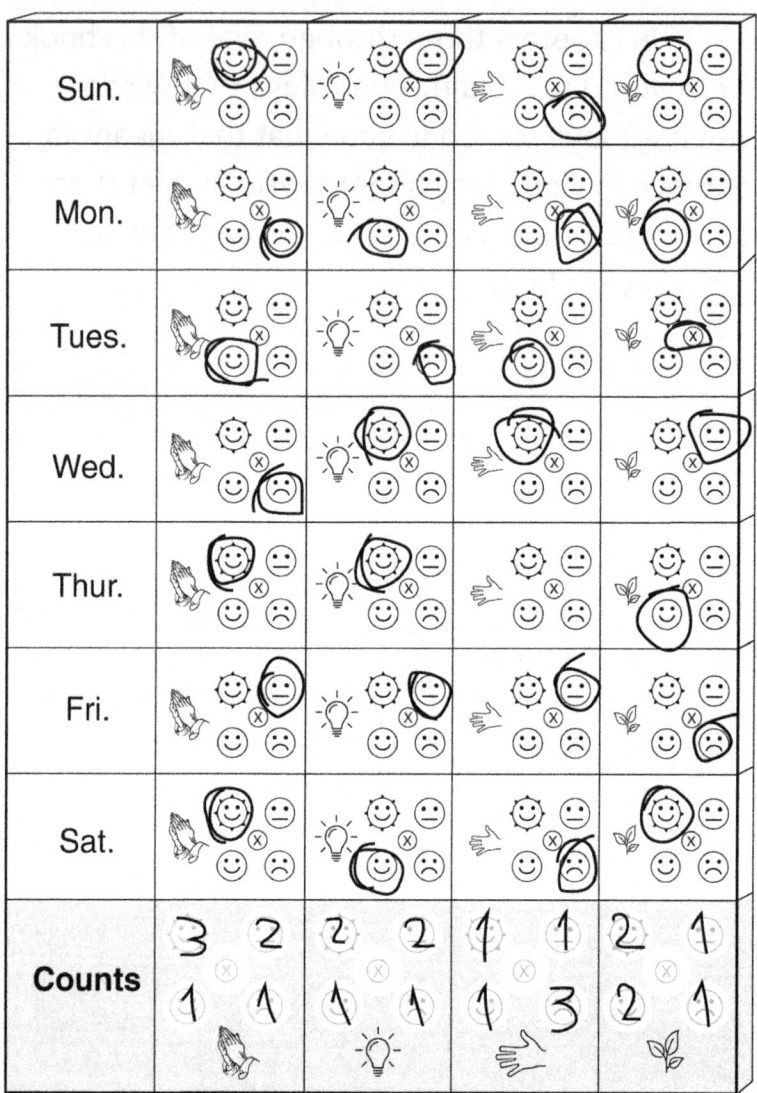

Sun.				
Mon.				
Tues.				
Wed.				
Thur.				
Fri.				
Sat.				
Counts	3 2 / 1 1	2 2 / 1 1	1 1 / 1 3	2 1 / 2 1

Keys:

☺ = Well done ☺ = Not yet
☺ = Sometimes ☹ = Could do better
Ⓧ = Choose this icon if the activity doesn't need to be done on this day

🙏 = Spent time with God
💡 = Light to someone in darkness
🌿 = Time with others growing in God
✋ = Helped/ministered to someone and/or took a Ministry Step

_____

_____

_____

_____

_____

_____

_____

_____

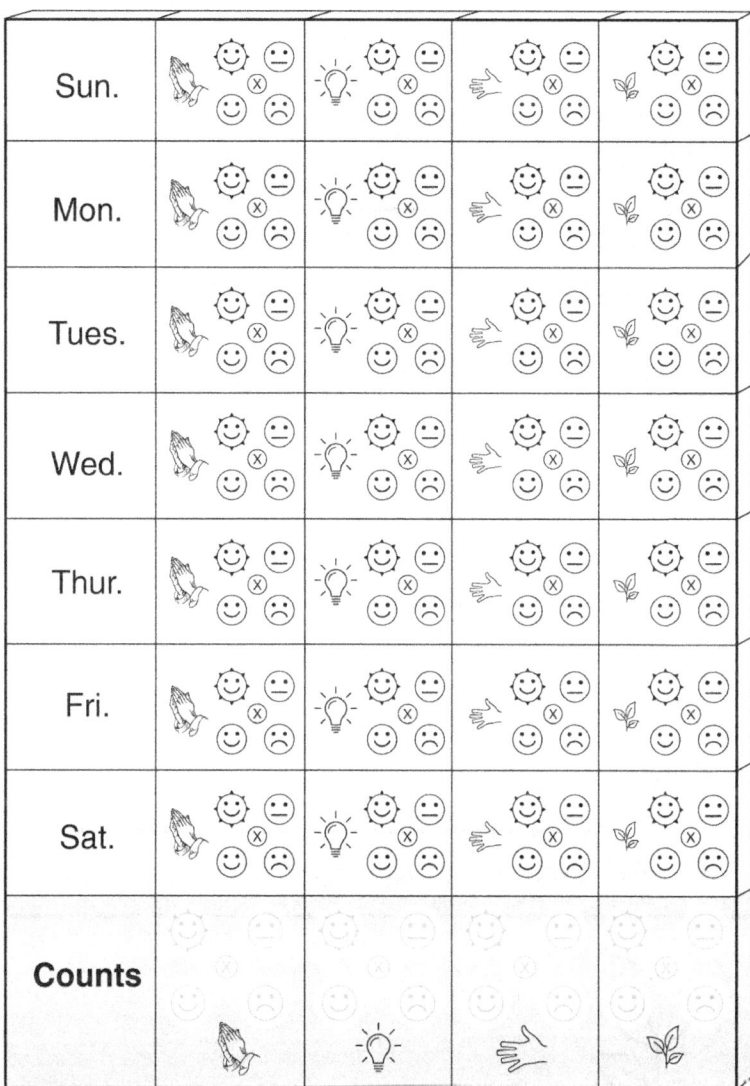

Keys:

☺ = Well done ☺ = Not yet

☺ = Sometimes ☹ = Could do better

Ⓧ = Choose this icon if the activity doesn't need to be done on this day

= Spent time with God

= Light to someone in darkness

= Time with others growing in God

= Helped/ministered to someone and/or took a Ministry Step

_____

_____

_____

_____

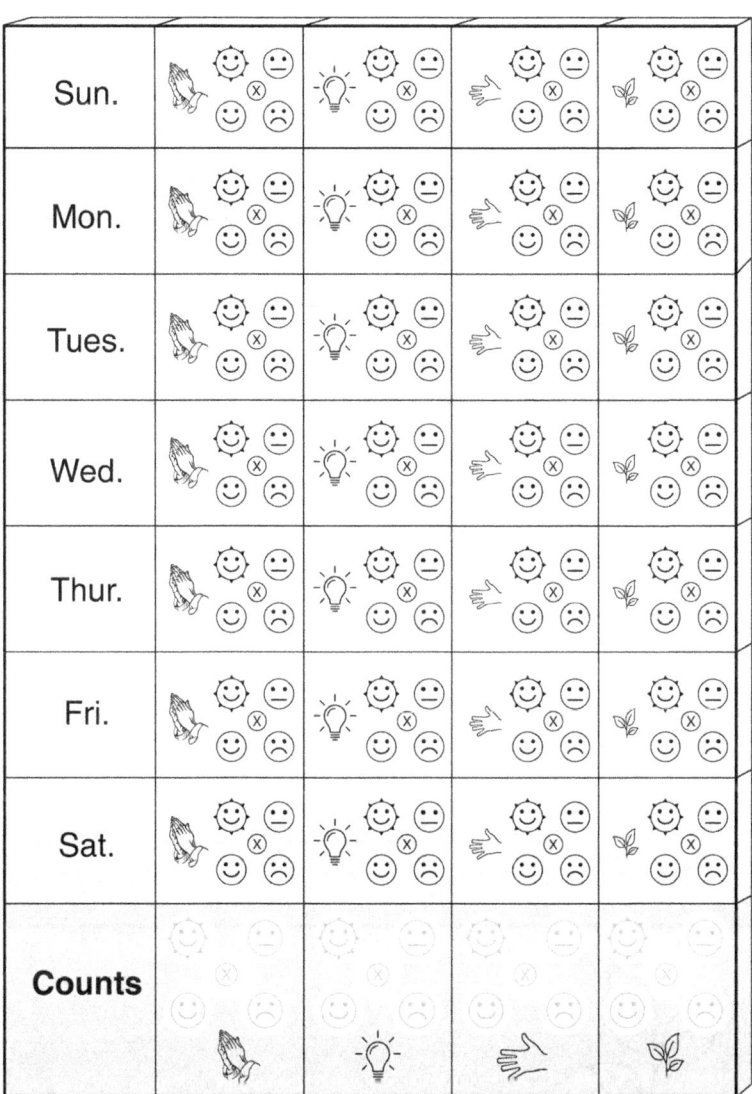

Sun.				
Mon.				
Tues.				
Wed.				
Thur.				
Fri.				
Sat.				
Counts				

Keys:

☺ = Well done   ☺ = Not yet

☺ = Sometimes   ☹ = Could do better

Ⓧ = Choose this icon if the activity doesn't need to be done on this day

🙏 = Spent time with God

💡 = Light to someone in darkness

🌱 = Time with others growing in God

🖐 = Helped/ministered to someone and/or took a Ministry Step

_____

_____

_____

_____

	🙏 Spent time with God	💡 Light to someone in darkness	✋ Helped/ministered to someone	🌱 Time with others growing in God
Sun.				
Mon.				
Tues.				
Wed.				
Thur.				
Fri.				
Sat.				
Counts				

Each cell contains the following selectable icons: ☺ Well done, ☺ Not yet, ☺ Sometimes, ☹ Could do better, and Ⓧ.

Keys:

☺ = Well done   ☺ = Not yet

☺ = Sometimes   ☹ = Could do better

Ⓧ = Choose this icon if the activity doesn't need to be done on this day

🙏 = Spent time with God

💡 = Light to someone in darkness

🌱 = Time with others growing in God

✋ = Helped/ministered to someone and/or took a Ministry Step

71

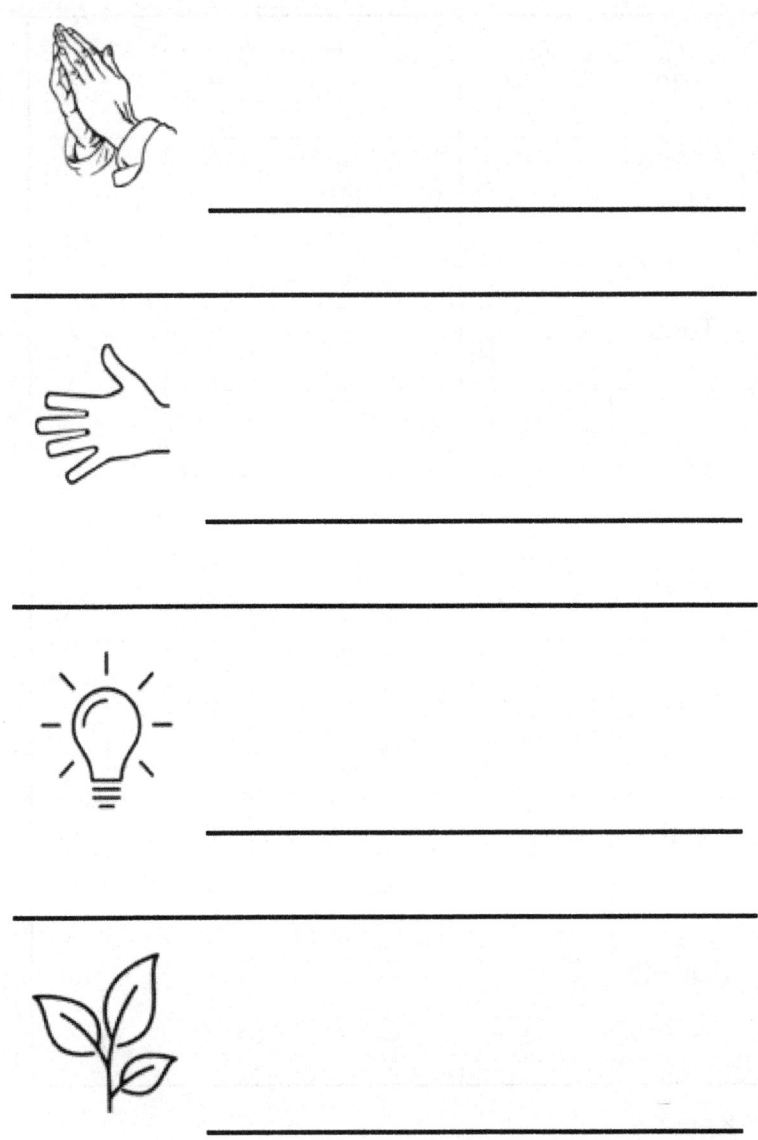

_____

_____

_____

_____

	Spent time with God	Light to someone in darkness	Helped/ministered to someone	Time with others growing in God
Sun.				
Mon.				
Tues.				
Wed.				
Thur.				
Fri.				
Sat.				
Counts				

Keys:

☺ = Well done   ☺ = Not yet

☺ = Sometimes   ☹ = Could do better

Ⓧ = Choose this icon if the activity doesn't need to be done on this day

= Spent time with God

= Light to someone in darkness

= Time with others growing in God

= Helped/ministered to someone and/or took a Ministry Step

_____

_____

_____

_____

Sun.	🙏 ☺ 😐 ☺ 😞 (x)	💡 ☺ 😐 ☺ 😞 (x)	🤲 ☺ 😐 ☺ 😞 (x)	🌿 ☺ 😐 ☺ 😞 (x)
Mon.	🙏 ☺ 😐 ☺ 😞 (x)	💡 ☺ 😐 ☺ 😞 (x)	🤲 ☺ 😐 ☺ 😞 (x)	🌿 ☺ 😐 ☺ 😞 (x)
Tues.	🙏 ☺ 😐 ☺ 😞 (x)	💡 ☺ 😐 ☺ 😞 (x)	🤲 ☺ 😐 ☺ 😞 (x)	🌿 ☺ 😐 ☺ 😞 (x)
Wed.	🙏 ☺ 😐 ☺ 😞 (x)	💡 ☺ 😐 ☺ 😞 (x)	🤲 ☺ 😐 ☺ 😞 (x)	🌿 ☺ 😐 ☺ 😞 (x)
Thur.	🙏 ☺ 😐 ☺ 😞 (x)	💡 ☺ 😐 ☺ 😞 (x)	🤲 ☺ 😐 ☺ 😞 (x)	🌿 ☺ 😐 ☺ 😞 (x)
Fri.	🙏 ☺ 😐 ☺ 😞 (x)	💡 ☺ 😐 ☺ 😞 (x)	🤲 ☺ 😐 ☺ 😞 (x)	🌿 ☺ 😐 ☺ 😞 (x)
Sat.	🙏 ☺ 😐 ☺ 😞 (x)	💡 ☺ 😐 ☺ 😞 (x)	🤲 ☺ 😐 ☺ 😞 (x)	🌿 ☺ 😐 ☺ 😞 (x)
Counts	☺ 😐 ☺ 😞 (x) 🙏	☺ 😐 ☺ 😞 (x) 💡	☺ 😐 ☺ 😞 (x) 🤲	☺ 😐 ☺ 😞 🌿

Keys:

☺ = Well done ☺ = Not yet
☺ = Sometimes 😞 = Could do better
(x) = Choose this icon if the activity doesn't need to be done on this day

🙏 = Spent time with God
💡 = Light to someone in darkness
🌿 = Time with others growing in God
🤲 = Helped/ministered to someone and/or took a Ministry Step

_____

_____

_____

_____

Sun.	🙏 ☺ 😐 ⊗ ☺ 😞	💡 ☺ 😐 ⊗ ☺ 😞	✋ ☺ 😐 ⊗ ☺ 😞	🌿 ☺ 😐 ⊗ ☺ 😞
Mon.	🙏 ☺ 😐 ⊗ ☺ 😞	💡 ☺ 😐 ⊗ ☺ 😞	✋ ☺ 😐 ⊗ ☺ 😞	🌿 ☺ 😐 ⊗ ☺ 😞
Tues.	🙏 ☺ 😐 ⊗ ☺ 😞	💡 ☺ 😐 ⊗ ☺ 😞	✋ ☺ 😐 ⊗ ☺ 😞	🌿 ☺ 😐 ⊗ ☺ 😞
Wed.	🙏 ☺ 😐 ⊗ ☺ 😞	💡 ☺ 😐 ⊗ ☺ 😞	✋ ☺ 😐 ⊗ ☺ 😞	🌿 ☺ 😐 ⊗ ☺ 😞
Thur.	🙏 ☺ 😐 ⊗ ☺ 😞	💡 ☺ 😐 ⊗ ☺ 😞	✋ ☺ 😐 ⊗ ☺ 😞	🌿 ☺ 😐 ⊗ ☺ 😞
Fri.	🙏 ☺ 😐 ⊗ ☺ 😞	💡 ☺ 😐 ⊗ ☺ 😞	✋ ☺ 😐 ⊗ ☺ 😞	🌿 ☺ 😐 ⊗ ☺ 😞
Sat.	🙏 ☺ 😐 ⊗ ☺ 😞	💡 ☺ 😐 ⊗ ☺ 😞	✋ ☺ 😐 ⊗ ☺ 😞	🌿 ☺ 😐 ⊗ ☺ 😞
Counts	🙏	💡	✋	🌿

Keys:

☺ = Well done   😐 = Not yet
☺ = Sometimes   😞 = Could do better
⊗ = Choose this icon if the activity doesn't
     need to be done on this day

🙏 = Spent time with God
💡 = Light to someone in darkness
🌿 = Time with others growing in God
✋ = Helped/ministered to someone
     and/or took a Ministry Step

_____

_____

_____

_____

	Spent time with God	Light to someone in darkness	Helped/ministered to someone and/or took a Ministry Step	Time with others growing in God
Sun.	🙏 ☺ 😐 ⓧ ☺ ☹	💡 ☺ 😐 ⓧ ☺ ☹	✋ ☺ 😐 ⓧ ☺ ☹	🌿 ☺ 😐 ⓧ ☺ ☹
Mon.	🙏 ☺ 😐 ⓧ ☺ ☹	💡 ☺ 😐 ⓧ ☺ ☹	✋ ☺ 😐 ⓧ ☺ ☹	🌿 ☺ 😐 ⓧ ☺ ☹
Tues.	🙏 ☺ 😐 ⓧ ☺ ☹	💡 ☺ 😐 ⓧ ☺ ☹	✋ ☺ 😐 ⓧ ☺ ☹	🌿 ☺ 😐 ⓧ ☺ ☹
Wed.	🙏 ☺ 😐 ⓧ ☺ ☹	💡 ☺ 😐 ⓧ ☺ ☹	✋ ☺ 😐 ⓧ ☺ ☹	🌿 ☺ 😐 ⓧ ☺ ☹
Thur.	🙏 ☺ 😐 ⓧ ☺ ☹	💡 ☺ 😐 ⓧ ☺ ☹	✋ ☺ 😐 ⓧ ☺ ☹	🌿 ☺ 😐 ⓧ ☺ ☹
Fri.	🙏 ☺ 😐 ⓧ ☺ ☹	💡 ☺ 😐 ⓧ ☺ ☹	✋ ☺ 😐 ⓧ ☺ ☹	🌿 ☺ 😐 ⓧ ☺ ☹
Sat.	🙏 ☺ 😐 ⓧ ☺ ☹	💡 ☺ 😐 ⓧ ☺ ☹	✋ ☺ 😐 ⓧ ☺ ☹	🌿 ☺ 😐 ⓧ ☺ ☹
Counts	☺ 😐 ⓧ ☺ ☹ 🙏	☺ 😐 ⓧ ☺ ☹ 💡	☺ 😐 ⓧ ☺ ☹ ✋	☺ 😐 ⓧ ☺ ☹ 🌿

Keys:

☺ = Well done   😐 = Not yet
☺ = Sometimes   ☹ = Could do better
ⓧ = Choose this icon if the activity doesn't need to be done on this day

🙏 = Spent time with God
💡 = Light to someone in darkness
🌿 = Time with others growing in God
✋ = Helped/ministered to someone and/or took a Ministry Step

_____

_____

_____

_____

80

	Spent time with God	Light to someone in darkness	Time with others growing in God	Helped/ministered to someone
Sun.				
Mon.				
Tues.				
Wed.				
Thur.				
Fri.				
Sat.				
Counts				

Keys:

☺ = Well done ☺ = Not yet
☺ = Sometimes ☹ = Could do better
(x) = Choose this icon if the activity doesn't need to be done on this day

= Spent time with God
= Light to someone in darkness
= Time with others growing in God
= Helped/ministered to someone and/or took a Ministry Step

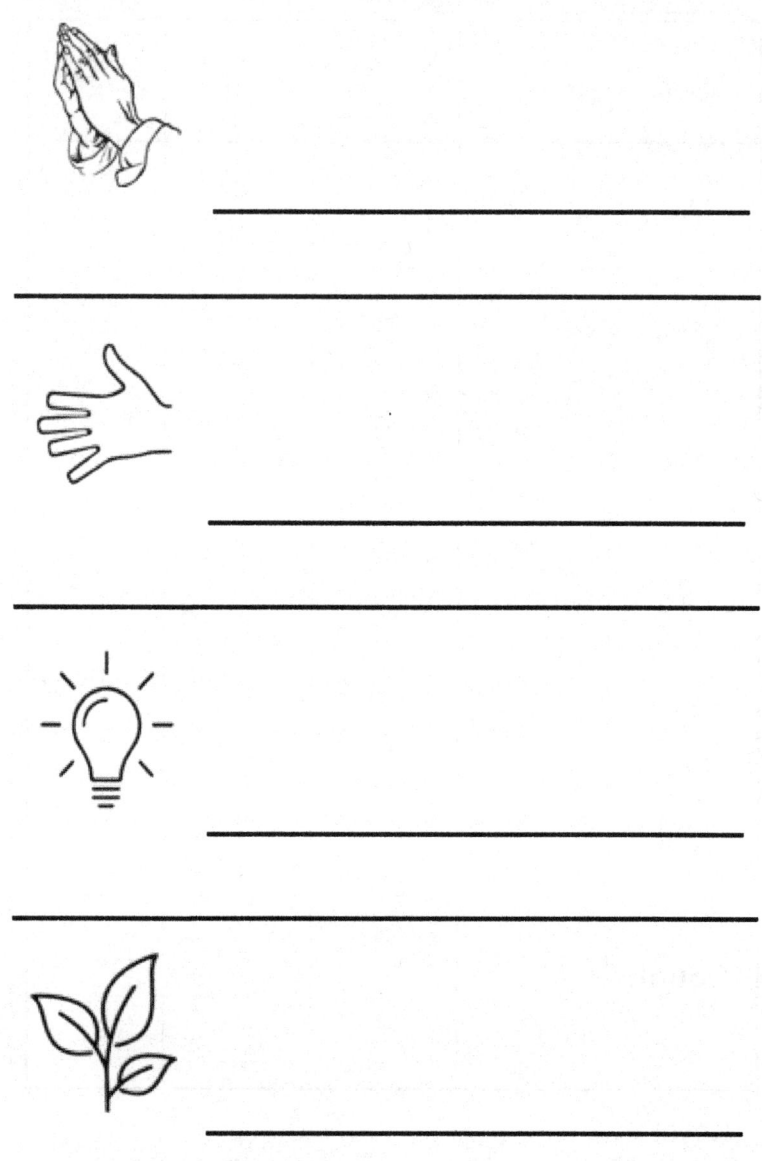

_____

_____

_____

_____

	Spent time with God	Light to someone in darkness	Time with others growing in God	Helped/ministered to someone
Sun.	☺ ☺ ☺ ☹ ⊗	☺ ☺ ☺ ☹ ⊗	☺ ☺ ☺ ☹ ⊗	☺ ☺ ☺ ☹ ⊗
Mon.	☺ ☺ ☺ ☹ ⊗	☺ ☺ ☺ ☹ ⊗	☺ ☺ ☺ ☹ ⊗	☺ ☺ ☺ ☹ ⊗
Tues.	☺ ☺ ☺ ☹ ⊗	☺ ☺ ☺ ☹ ⊗	☺ ☺ ☺ ☹ ⊗	☺ ☺ ☺ ☹ ⊗
Wed.	☺ ☺ ☺ ☹ ⊗	☺ ☺ ☺ ☹ ⊗	☺ ☺ ☺ ☹ ⊗	☺ ☺ ☺ ☹ ⊗
Thur.	☺ ☺ ☺ ☹ ⊗	☺ ☺ ☺ ☹ ⊗	☺ ☺ ☺ ☹ ⊗	☺ ☺ ☺ ☹ ⊗
Fri.	☺ ☺ ☺ ☹ ⊗	☺ ☺ ☺ ☹ ⊗	☺ ☺ ☺ ☹ ⊗	☺ ☺ ☺ ☹ ⊗
Sat.	☺ ☺ ☺ ☹ ⊗	☺ ☺ ☺ ☹ ⊗	☺ ☺ ☺ ☹ ⊗	☺ ☺ ☺ ☹ ⊗
Counts				

Keys:

☺ = Well done   ☺ = Not yet

☺ = Sometimes   ☹ = Could do better

⊗ = Choose this icon if the activity doesn't need to be done on this day

🙏 = Spent time with God

💡 = Light to someone in darkness

🌱 = Time with others growing in God

✋ = Helped/ministered to someone and/or took a Ministry Step

_____

_____

_____

_____

	Spent time with God	Light to someone in darkness	Time with others growing in God	Helped/ministered to someone
Sun.				
Mon.				
Tues.				
Wed.				
Thur.				
Fri.				
Sat.				
Counts				

Keys:

☺ = Well done   ☺ = Not yet

☺ = Sometimes   ☹ = Could do better

Ⓧ = Choose this icon if the activity doesn't need to be done on this day

🙏 = Spent time with God

💡 = Light to someone in darkness

🌱 = Time with others growing in God

🖐 = Helped/ministered to someone and/or took a Ministry Step

KingdomStandards.com

Standards We Share as Disciples

I worship the one God.

The God of Abraham, Isaac and Jacob. The Father, Son, and Holy Spirit are the one true God. God is the Creator of the Universe, Earth and Man.

The Old Covenant.

The First Covenant began with Abraham and extended to His seed. God gave Moses the Law, which is perfect. The Law requires all lawbreakers to die and thus leads people to salvation described in the New Covenant because we are all lawbreakers.

The New Covenant.

God sent Jesus, His Son. Jesus was born of a virgin, fully God and fully man, yet without sin. Jesus, our

Savior, came as a perfect lamb to save us by taking the punishment of death prescribed by the Law. God raised Him from death. Jesus is the Way, Truth and the Life, the only way to the Father. Jesus knew my name when I was in my mother's womb and calls me to live for Him. By grace through faith, I experience His salvation by answering His call, making Jesus my Savior and Lord. At salvation I am reconciled to God by receiving Jesus' payment for the wrongs I've done. I am adopted as a child of God.

The Kingdom.

When I experience salvation, I die with Christ. I am transferred from the kingdom of darkness to His Kingdom of peace and righteousness. I become part of Him, His bride and a citizen of the Kingdom. In the beginning, God created us male and female and established marriage between male and female. I am faithful in marriage and I care for my family. I gather with and love other Christ-followers as the family of God. We love others, teaching all things Jesus commanded and extend salvation so others can be transferred into the Kingdom of God.

The Spirit and the Word.

Jesus is the Word of God. God's Word is perfect. I feed on the Word and commit myself to Biblical literacy, learning and faithfully following His teachings and defending Truth. I welcome God, the Holy Spirit, as the Comforter and Guide Christ gives.

The One Baptism.

I have been baptized into Christ by faith, making Him Lord. I chose to die to myself and live for Christ, yielding myself, my time, money and resources to Him. I cannot serve God and myself, money or any other thing. I cannot consider myself on the path to Heaven when living unrepentantly, doing wrong things. I recognize I have been forgiven and forgive, fulfilling the ministry of reconciliation that He calls us to. I welcome the Holy Spirit to immerse me-providing His power to live a righteous life of love, peace & holiness, & to witness & to be fruitful serving others with the gifts God has given me.

ABOUT MICHAEL COULSON

Michael Coulson is the lead pastor of People's EC Church in Lehighton, PA and The Echo online campus. Pastor Mike has been married to his wife Laura for over a decade and they have been blessed with 3 wonderful children: Levi, Brooks, and Grace.

Pastor Mike and Laura met the first week of college at Millersville University where he graduated with a bachelor's degree in Finance with a minor in Athletic Coaching. He received his Master of Divinity degree from Kairos University.

In his spare time, Pastor Mike loves to play with his kids, coach baseball and soccer, play bass, watch cycling, and read. He is the author of "Becoming Jesus' Apprentice."

www.peoplesecchurch.com

Made in the USA
Middletown, DE
02 June 2024

55066144R00056